EARTH

metamorphic rocks

NATIONAL GEOGRAPHIC NATURE LIBRARY

EARTH

NATIONAL GEOGRAPHIC NATURE LIBRARY

by Patricia Daniels

NATIONAL GEOGRAPHIC SOCIETY

Washington, D.C.

*All photographs supplied by the
Earth Scenes Division of
Animals Animals Enterprises*

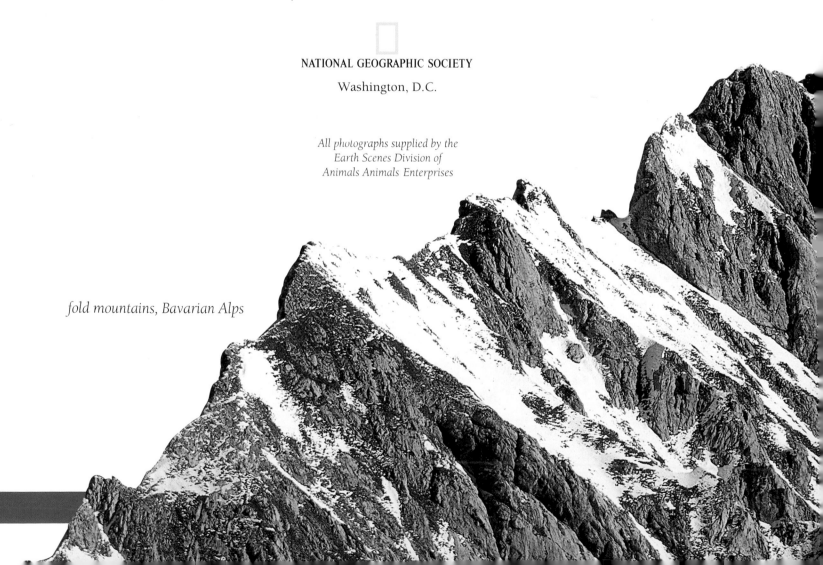

fold mountains, Bavarian Alps

Table of Contents

topaz

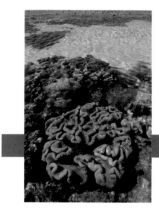

coral reef, Australia

ice sheet, Antarctica

sand dunes, Namib Desert

*active volcano,
Mount Shishaldin, Alaska*

*prairie flower,
North Dakota*

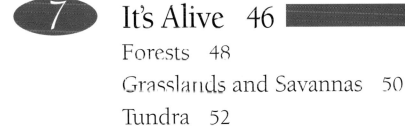

*rock formation,
Nevada*

WHAT IS THE EARTH?

Imagine that you are a visitor from outer space. What does your guidebook tell you about the Earth? Let's see—it is the third planet from a medium-size sun. At four and a half billion years old, it is a middle-aged world. It contains so much water that it appears blue from space.

What else do we know about this blue planet? Our guidebook has some more facts about the Earth:

- It is SPHERICAL (SFEAR-ih-kuhl), or shaped like a ball.
- It is 7,926 MILES WIDE at its widest point.
- OCEANS cover more than two-thirds of its surface.
- If you could slice it in half, you would see THREE LAYERS: the CRUST, the MANTLE, and the CORE.
- The outer layer of the planet is broken into HUGE PIECES that are always moving.

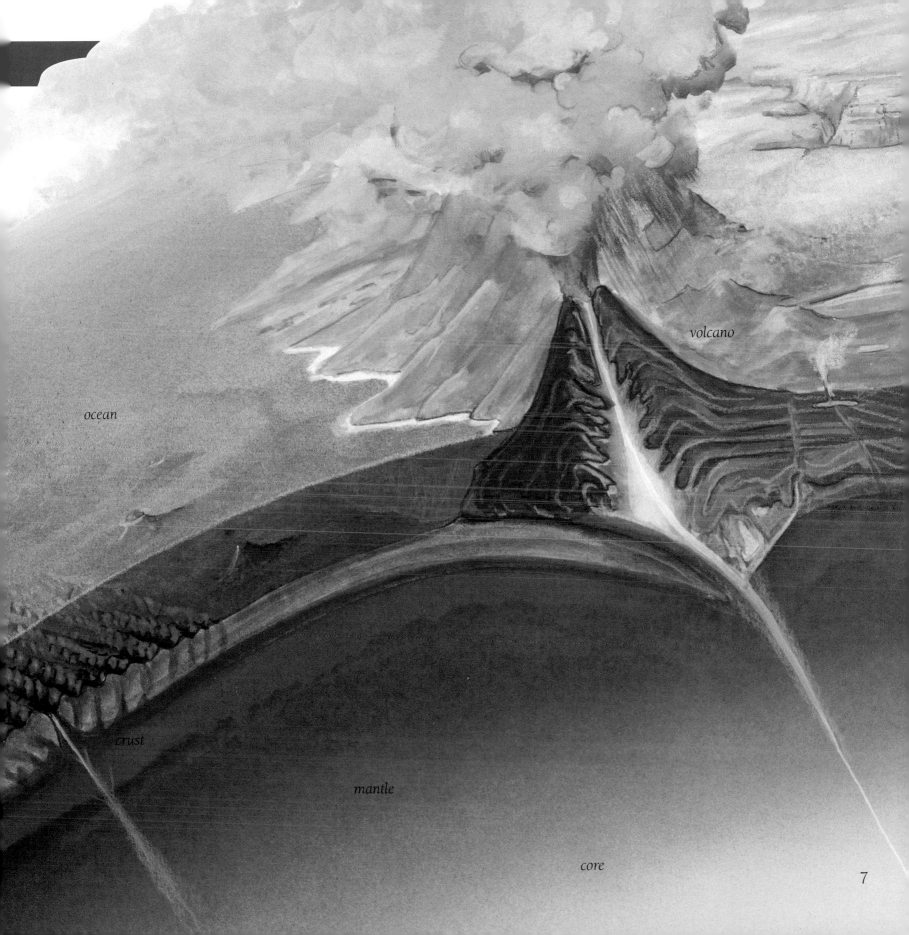

volcano

ocean

crust

mantle

core

Moving and Building

Does the ground feel steady under your feet? It's not! Under a carpet of soil, the Earth's surface is broken into huge, rocky plates. These plates hold the ocean floor and the dry land. You can't feel it, but the plates are moving. Slowly, over millions of years, they pull the land around like an ever changing puzzle. The plates touch each other. Sometimes the edge of one plate dives under the edge of another. Other plates pull apart. Where plates meet, volcanoes erupt, mountains rise, and earthquakes shake the ground.

FOLDED AND MOLDED
Squeezed by moving plates, this layered rock rumpled like wet laundry.

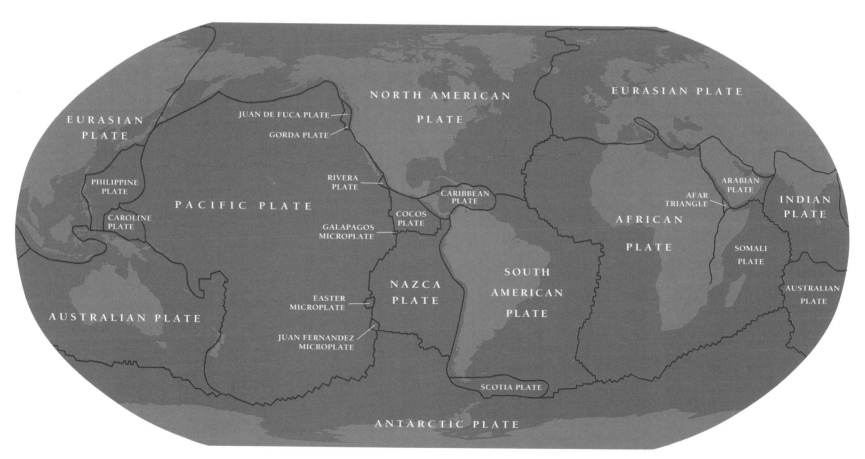

THE BIG EARTH JIGSAW PUZZLE
The outer shell of the Earth is broken into seven big plates and a number of smaller ones. Scientists think the plates may be pushed around by intense heat from deep inside the Earth.

SMASHING ALPS

The Alps, a famous mountain range in Europe, were formed tens of millions of years ago. They were born when the African plate smacked into the Eurasian plate. Where the two plates collided, the ground wrinkled up into mountains.

GREAT BALLS OF FIRE

Hot, melted rock called lava (LAH-vuh) erupts from the ground in Iceland. Two plates are pulling apart under that island. As the plates separate, melted rock from deep within the Earth, called magma (MAG-muh), sprays out through the crack. When magma reaches the Earth's surface, it is called lava. Lava cools and hardens into rock, making new land.

WHOSE FAULT IS IT?

This scar-like valley is the San Andreas Fault in California. The valley occurs where two plates meet. As the plates move in opposite directions, they rub together and cause earthquakes.

Earth's Makeup

Three kinds of rocks are found in the planet's crust. Igneous (IG-nee-us) rocks are made of cooled magma, which is itself made of melted rock. Sedimentary (sed-uh-MEN-tuh-ree) rocks are formed from sand, mud, and other particles carried in rivers and streams. Metamorphic (met-uh-MOR-fik) rocks started off as igneous or sedimentary rocks. Then forces under the Earth's surface squeezed and heated them until they changed form.

gneiss

Metamorphic rocks are made from other rocks that are squeezed and heated inside the Earth.

obsidian

ROCK TALK

Gneiss (NICE) is a metamorphic rock. Obsidian (uhb-SID-ee-uhn), a glassy, igneous rock, forms from lava. Limestone, a sedimentary rock, is striped with layers of limey mud.

limestone

ROCK BASICS

The three kinds of rocks on Earth are made from minerals; they are the building blocks of all rocks. There are hundreds of different kinds of minerals. Some, such as this topaz, are called gems (JEMZ) and are used in jewelry. Gems, often found inside rocks, are hard and shiny. They have smooth, regular shapes.

BEARLY ESCAPING ▶

Rising into the Wyoming sky, Devil's Tower is a giant mass of igneous rock. Indian legend says that it started as a tree stump, then grew when seven girls climbed on it to escape from a bear.

10

Surface Shapers

The really big shapes on Earth—mountains, ocean basins, continents—are built by moving plates. The plates are probably powered by heat from inside the planet. The smaller parts of our landscape, from the Grand Canyon to the boulder in your backyard, are carved by forces on the Earth's surface. These forces include wind, water, ice, and gravity, which is the force of a planet that pulls things toward its center. Gravity is the force that holds you onto the ground and makes pebbles roll downhill.

CARVING A CAVE
This cave in Brazil used to be solid underground rock. The rock, called limestone, dissolves in water. Rainwater that soaked down from above became an underground stream. That stream dissolved the limestone, hollowing out a cave.

BIG, COLD BULLDOZER
Dragged downhill by gravity, a glacier at Canada's Lake Louise chews right through mountains to make a U-shaped valley. This huge river of ice slowly scrapes smooth rock walls.

FARMERS ARE POWERFUL
All over the world, people are changing the shape of the Earth by plowing and planting.

A RIVER DELIVERS
Even a shallow river, like this one in the Great Smoky Mountains, can shape rock. When streams like this flood, sand and pebbles carried in the water carve away at the riverbed.

NE GOLDEN ARCH
day this sandstone arch stands free inst the sky. Once it was part of a ge layer of rock. Wind and water re away—or eroded—the softer rounding rock and left the more istant arch behind.

13

1 The Deep Blue Sea

Even though different oceans have different names, such as the Atlantic or the Pacific, they are really connected and form one big ocean. Earth's ocean holds more than 32 million cubic miles of water. Under this water is a hidden world. Towering mountains and deep valleys form a dark landscape unseen by most human eyes.

PASS THE SALT, PLEASE
Have you ever tried to drink seawater? Yuck! The ocean is way too salty to drink. That's because streams and rivers dissolve salt from rocks and soil in their beds. They add this salt to the seawater when they flow into the ocean.

RECYCLED OCEANS

Most of the water in today's oceans and rivers was formed four billion years ago. In the planet's early days, the Earth was hot and dry. Then volcanoes released gases, including water vapor, from inside the planet. When the water vapor cooled, it changed into rain. It splashed down to make the water we drink today.

BREAKING NEWS

The ocean may break into pounding surf where it meets the shore. Water carves away land in one place. Waves carry off sand and rocks and deposit them elsewhere, building new land.

THE BIG HEAT PUMP

Without the ocean, the Earth would be bone-chillingly cold, like Mars. Water absorbs heat more easily than land does. The ocean soaks up heat from the sun in summer. In the winter, it releases the heat slowly into the air, keeping the planet warm.

A Shore Thing

Continents don't stop at the ocean's edge. They keep going underwater, reaching out for miles along what's called the continental shelf. The shallow, sunny waters of the continental shelf are home to most of the ocean's animals and plants. Corals build their colorful cities there. Seaweed sways in the currents. Waves pound the shore, crunching rock into perfect wet sand for sand castles.

LOBSTER LAND
A spiny lobster blends in well with i[?] brilliant underwater home near Hawaii. Coastal waters are rich in plants and sea creatures.

THE CORAL CONNECTION
Coral reefs grow in water no more than 150 feet deep. Large reefs can protect the coast from rough waves.

WAVE GOOD-BYE
When a wave rolls toward shore, the water is not moving forward. Waves get their shapes when water particles roll around like spinning logs under the water's surface. The water on the surface just bobs up and down. The shape of the wave is what moves through the water. As the wave nears land, water particles under the surface hit shore, and the circular motion tosses the water onto the land.

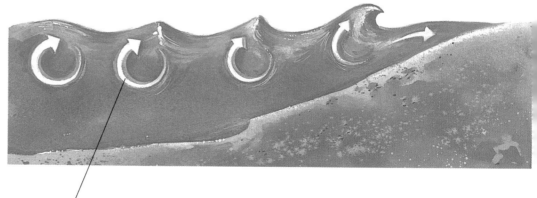

A wave breaks, or topples over on itself, as it reaches shore.

NO SWIMMING ▶
This rough Scottish cliff, home to seabirds, may have been completely underwater when sea levels were higher. Now it is exposed to wind and waves that crack and crumble the rock.

Way Down Deep

Dive down, down into the ocean. Leave the sunlit waters behind and visit the ocean floor, 6,000 to 20,000 feet below the surface. The deepest parts of the ocean are dark and cold. The weight of the water presses down with tremendous force. Even here, there is life and change.

AT HOME IN THE DEPTHS

The deep ocean is home to some of the strangest animals in the world. Some are blind. Some have lights on their bodies to attract prey. Others, such as tube worms, are attached to the ocean floor. In parts of the deep ocean, the ocean floor opens where two plates are separating. Lava slowly leaks out. Nearby, mineral chimneys—called black smokers—release smoke and hot water from inside the Earth.

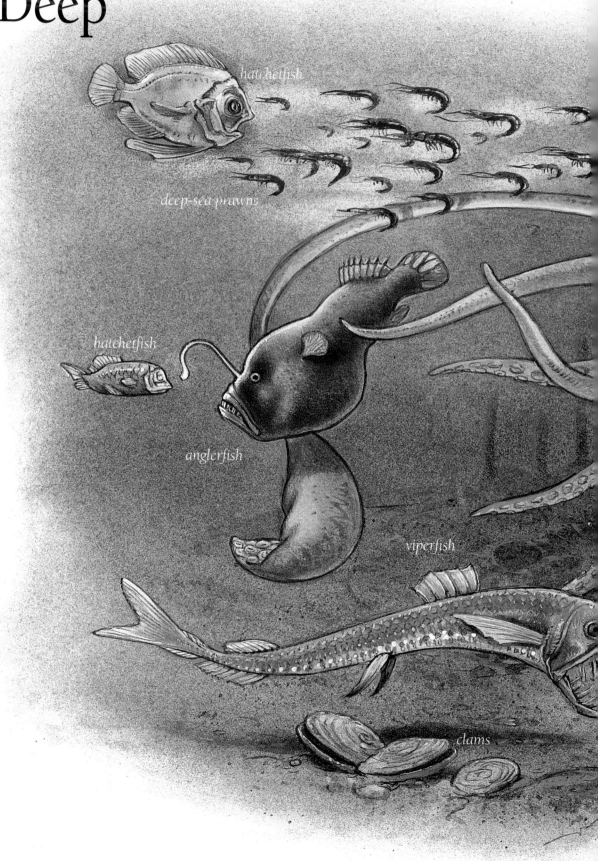

hatchetfish

deep-sea prawns

hatchetfish

anglerfish

viperfish

clams

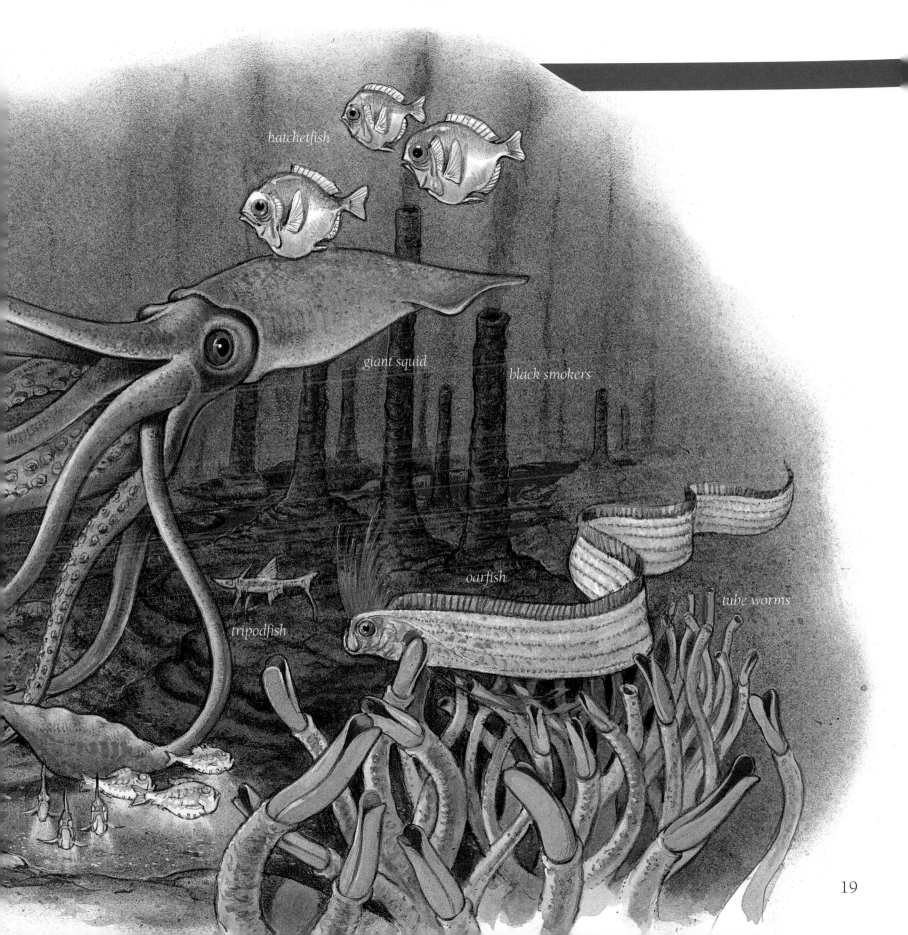

hatchetfish

giant squid

black smokers

oarfish

tube worms

tripodfish

19

2 Islands

Any body of land surrounded by water is an island. That is, unless it's so big it gets promoted to a continent. Australia is large enough to be a continent, for instance. Greenland, less than one third the size of Australia, is an island. It is called a continental island because it once was attached to a continent. Other kinds of islands are called oceanic, coral, or barrier, depending on how they were formed.

JUST BIG ENOUGH FOR ONE TREE
Little Livingstone Island, off the coast of Guatemala is home only to birds. Little Livingstone is a continental island. It used to be part of the continent of North America.

ISLAND TREASURES
Barrier islands, such as the Outer Banks of North Carolina where pirates once hid, are long and narrow. Barrier islands, built by waves moving sand and gravel along the shore for a long time, protect the coast from storms.

VOLCANIC BIRTH
Oceanic islands, like these near Hawaii, are really the tops of old volcanoes. They reach down to the ocean floor. Plants may cover their slopes and people can live there in safety now that the islands no longer erupt.

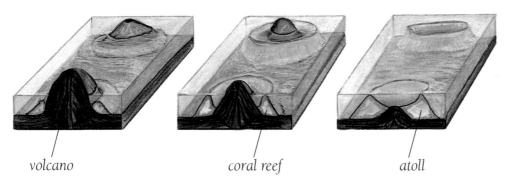

CORAL CROWN

Atolls are ring-shaped islands made of coral. The coral grew around the top of a volcano that sank back into the ocean.

volcano

coral reef

atoll

An Island Is Born

If you had been sailing near Iceland in 1963, you would have seen an island burst from the sea in clouds of ash and steam. Surtsey, as the newborn island was named, showed that a volcanic island can be built from ash and lava in just days.

Some volcanoes, such as the ones that make up the Hawaiian Islands, rise over hot spots, areas where magma wells up and burns through Earth's crust.

LAVA LIFE
Ferns find toeholds in cooled Hawaiian lava. This ropy-looking rock is called pahoehoe (pa-HOY-hoy).

HOT DAY AT THE BEACH ▶
Lava pours into the ocean, adding new land to the Hawaiian coast. The Hawaiian islands are a chain of volcanoes. Old ones are now sinking under their own weight. New ones are being born underwater.

THAR SHE BLOWS
Lava and ash rising from the Mid-Atlantic Ridge built the island of Surtsey. The ridge marks the crack where two plates separated under the Atlantic Ocean.

Surtsey

3 Waterworks

We live in a wet world. Water falls from the sky as rain, hail, sleet, and snow. Water sweeps down mountains in rivers. Ponds and streams give frogs and fish homes, while lakes hold swans and shipwrecks. Water flows under the ground, too. In fact, there is 30 times as much groundwater in the world as there is surface water. Luckily, almost all surface and groundwater is fresh, not salty. Otherwise, we would get thirsty fast!

If all Earth's water were shown in this picture, the bathtub would contain the oceans, which hold more than 97 percent of the water. A glass of ice represents the glaciers, which hold about 2 percent. A tiny cup represents the rivers and lakes, which hold less than one percent of the world's water.

WATER TRANSPORT
Rivers, like this one in Wales, carry rainwater and melting snow from mountaintops toward the sea.

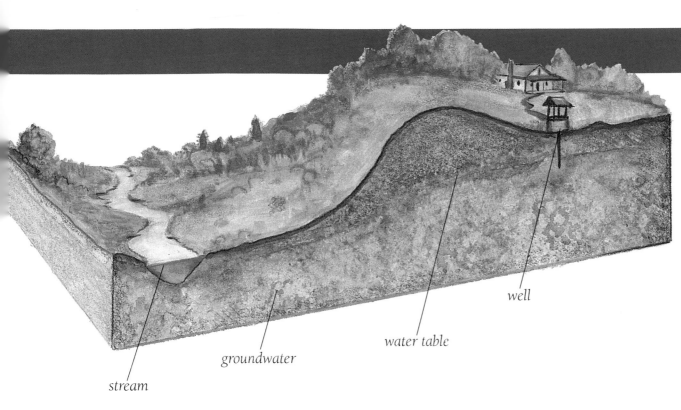

SECRET WATER

Rainwater trickles down through the soil. It soaks into the rocks and dirt underground until the spaces between the rocks are filled with water. This sunken water is called groundwater. The part of the groundwater closest to the surface is called the water table.

well

water table

groundwater

stream

Rivers

Compared to the ocean, rivers are dinky. Even the biggest ones—the Amazon, the Nile, and the Yangtze—carry only a tiny amount of the world's water. Yet to humans, rivers are all-important. They give us food for our dinners. They are roads for our boats. Rivers connect us to each other. That's why many of the world's great cities, such as New York, London, and Shanghai, grew up on rivers.

Huge crocodiles live on the banks of the Nile River.

The D River in Oregon is only 121 feet long. It is the world's shortest river.

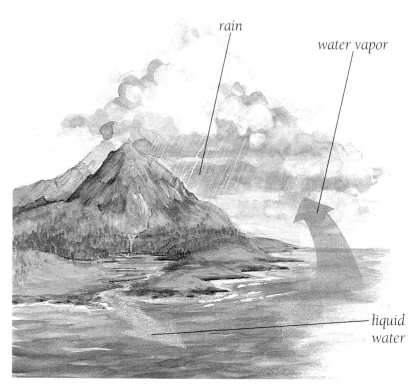

rain

water vapor

liquid water

THE WATER CYCLE

Powered by heat from the sun, water moves in an endless cycle between ocean, air, and land. Heat turns ocean, lake, and river water into vapor. The vapor rises into the air. In time, it condenses, or clumps together into clouds of water droplets. When the vapor cools, it turns into liquid water again, and rain falls onto the land and oceans, completing the cycle.

RIVER'S END

Like mighty rivers around the world, the Mississippi River spreads out lazily into a watery plain where it flows into the ocean. The plain is called a delta. The 2,340-mile-long Mississippi is North America's biggest river.

YOURS 'TIL NIAGARA FALLS

Now here's an obvious name: Niagara Falls is where the Niagara River falls! Waterfalls like this one occur where rivers drop over a hard, rocky ledge. Niagara Falls is 20 miles from Lake Erie, on the border between New York State and Canada. The immense force of the falling water is slowly wearing away the rock underneath. One day—in about 20,000 years—the moving water will wear the rock all the way back to Lake Erie, draining the lake completely.

COUNTRY-SIZE RIVER

A tracing of the Amazon River System laid over a drawing of the 48 continental United States reveals how vast an area the system covers.

27

Weird Water

Water under the ground is a sunken treasure. Small farms and great cities tap into it for drinking water. Usually groundwater is clear and cold. In some places, though, it flows next to rocks warmed by magma or hot gases. These rocks heat the water. Then it may come to the surface as a bubbling hot spring—or as a geyser (GUY-zur), an erupting fountain of boiling water.

BLOWING OFF STEAM
A geyser in Yellowstone National Park lets loose with a blast of super-hot water.

THAT SINKING FEELING
The city of Tokyo is sinking. In places, its streets are 14 feet below sea level. Tokyo's eight million people have been using up the groundwater under the city. As the groundwater is pumped away, the ground sinks under heavy buildings. Other cities, such as Los Angeles, have the same problem.

BOILING BATHTUBS

Don't bring your rubber ducky to this hot bath! Hot springs, like this one in Kenya, range in temperature from warm to blistering. Heated to the boiling point underground, the water seeps up through cracks to the surface. There, it forms steaming pools. Hot springs and geysers are usually found in volcanic areas.

Ice Blankets

Just 18,000 years ago—practically yesterday in Earth time—one-third of the planet was covered with ice. Much of this chilly coating has melted away, but ice still covers one-tenth of the Earth. Some takes the form of glaciers, rivers of ice that slowly flow down mountainsides. The rest is locked into ice sheets on the island of Greenland and the continent of Antarctica.

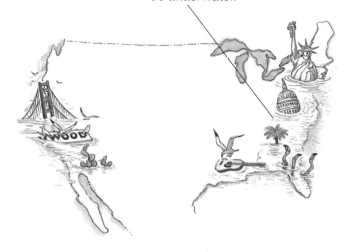

If the Antarctic ice sheet melted, the world sea level would rise by almost 200 feet. Almost all the cities on the U.S. coasts would be underwater.

ICE ATTACK
This Alaskan glacier is calving, which means chunks of ice are breaking off the front of the glacier. The huge chunks are new icebergs. Glaciers are built from compacted snow. Pulled by gravity, the glacier slides downhill. Most glaciers are slow, moving only a few inches a day. But some gallop at more than 150 feet daily.

LOOK OUT BELOW!
When dealing with an iceberg, what you don't see can hurt you. As much as seven-eighths of an iceberg is hidden below the surface of the water.

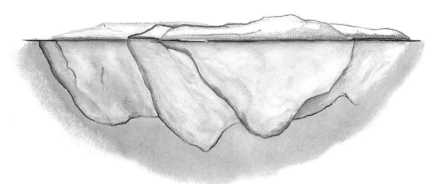

COLD COUNTRY
Visitors to Antarctica get a cold welcome. An ice sheet covers most of the continent. It holds almost all the world's ice and two-thirds of its fresh water.

30

4 Dry Spells

When you think of a desert, do you think of sand? Head-pounding heat? Camels? Many deserts have all of those things, but some don't. Deserts can be cold, icy, and rocky. They can even suffer dangerous floods. Any place that gets fewer than ten inches of rain a year is a desert. There are five kinds of deserts: subtropical, coastal, rain shadow, interior, and polar. Each kind is dry for a different reason.

HOT ROCK

Ayers Rock looms over the subtropical Australian desert like a sleeping giant. Subtropical deserts are found in warm lands not far from the Equator. Wet, hot air rises near the Equator, then cools and drops its moisture as tropical rains. By the time the winds reach the subtropics north and south of the Equator, they are dry, and little rain falls.

DRIER THAN DUST

The Atacama Desert of Peru is the world's driest place. Parts of it get less than .02 inch of moisture a year. The Atacama is a coastal desert. Coastal deserts occur in areas where cold seawater along a coast chills the air, and the cold air forms fog, but not rain clouds.

rain clouds

rain shadow

IN THE SHADOW OF RAIN

Mountains steal the rain from rain shadow deserts. As a wet wind blows up a mountainside, the air cools. The water it contains condenses into rain clouds, and the rain drops on the near side of the mountain. The other side—in the rain shadow—stays dry.

DRY ICE

Antarctica is a polar desert, even though much of the world's water lies frozen on its surface. In fact, Antarctica is the driest continent on Earth. The air is so cold there that it can't hold much moisture.

Interior deserts, such as the Taklimakan of China, are found in the center of continents. Interior deserts are dry because they are so far from oceans that no moisture is left in the winds that reach them.

33

Sandtastic

Great beach—but where's the water? Sandy deserts are found around the world, particularly in Africa and Asia. Some have dunes that tower 300 feet high. These lands were once green and lush. Then the climate changed. The plants died, and the soil blew away. The rock slowly broke down into sand.

OFFICIAL SAND
According to geologists, only bits of rock smaller than the "o" in this sentence can be called sand. Any larger, and rock pieces are called gravel.

THE FOGGY DESERT
The Namib Desert in southern Africa gets plenty of fog, but almost no rain. Mist rolls in each morning from the nearby Atlantic Ocean.

The desert's hot air sometimes makes faraway objects look like they're floating. This kind of floating image is called a mirage (mih-RAJH).

DESERT TREASURE
In even the driest deserts, pools of water may seep up from underground. These life-giving places are called oases (oh-AY-sees).

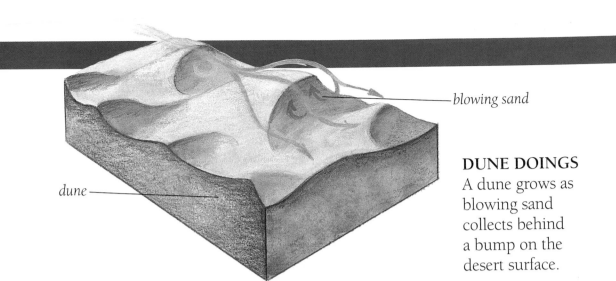

blowing sand

dune

ON THE MOVE
Hot winds blow dunes across the desert. Without plants to slow the wind, dunes can travel hundreds of feet each year.

DUNE DOINGS
A dune grows as blowing sand collects behind a bump on the desert surface.

5 Mountains

If you could watch a movie of the Earth's history on fast-forward speed, you would see three kinds of mountains growing. Where plates collide, the land would wrinkle up like an old bath mat, forming fold mountains. Fault-block mountains would rise where plates pull apart. Volcanic mountains would build from eruptions.

HOW HIGH CAN YOU GO?

To some mountain climbers, reaching a peak is the ultimate challenge. They try to climb the highest mountains on each continent. These peaks range from Asia's rugged Mount Everest, tallest in the world, to the gentler Mount Kosciusko in Australia.

IT'S A SQUEEZE

Ribbons of colorful rock zigzag along a mountainside in Utah. This landscape was formed when two plates collided, folding the rocks into mountains.

Mount Everest
Asia

Mount McKinley
North America

Mount Aconcagua
South America

Mount Kiliman
Africa

El'Brus
Europe

Vinson Massif
Antarctica

Mount Kosciusko
Australia

BIG GREEN WRINKLES

Folding also built the gently rolling hills of the Shenandoah Mountains.

fault

GOING UP!

Fault-block mountains occur when large pieces of crust—the Earth's rocky outer layer—tilt sideways as a plate is pulled apart. Fault-block mountains usually have one steep side and one gently sloping side.

The Cascade Mountains run for 700 miles from Canada to northern California. The range still contains active volcanoes.

THERE'S A FIRE INSIDE

This snowy peak in Oregon's Cascade Mountains was once an active volcano.

The Roof of the World

Reaching higher than some airplanes can fly, the Himalaya form the tallest mountain range in the world. This sky-scraping Asian mountain chain runs through northern India, Nepal, and Tibet. It contains the five tallest peaks in the world.

TAKE A DEEP BREATH
The tallest Himalayan peaks reach into very thin air. Climbers there usually carry bottles of oxygen. They learn to go up slowly, allowing their bodies to adjust to the elevation.

Air at the peak of Mount Everest has only one-third as much oxygen as air at sea level.

THE BIG ONE
The Tibetans call it Chomolungma, "Mother-Goddess of the World." Mount Everest, in the central Himalaya, is 29,028 feet tall. When you stand on its peak, you are higher than anything else on the planet.

YOUNG 'UNS

As mountains go, the rugged Himalaya are fairly young. They are only 40 or 50 million years old. Wind and water will wear down their rough edges. Over time they will grow to look like North America's Appalachian Mountains, which are 460 million years old.

CONTINENTAL CRACK-UP

CRASH! About 40 to 60 million years ago, the plate carrying India began to smash into the Asian plate. Where the plates met, the land crumpled into the Himalayan mountains. The leading edge of India continues to dive beneath the Asian plate today. It raises the Himalayan land by one inch every five years.

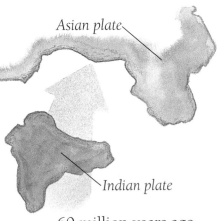

Asian plate

Indian plate

60 million years ago

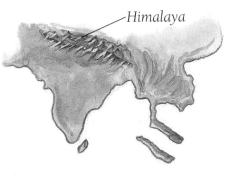

Himalaya

today

39

What a Blast!

Right now, somewhere in the world, a volcano is erupting. Wherever the Earth's plates pull apart, or where one plate slides under another, burning hot magma rises toward the Earth's surface. In some places, the magma builds a volcano. Volcanoes can even grow when magma burns through the middle of a plate at a place called a hot spot.

A HOT DAY IN THE ISLANDS
Hawaii's Mount Kilauea is one of the Earth's most active volcanoes. All of the Hawaiian islands are volcanoes. They formed over a hot spot beneath the Pacific Ocean.

40

ISLAND BYE-BYE

In 1883, a volcanic island in Indonesia called Krakatau blew itself up. All three of its volcanic peaks exploded, causing a tidal wave that killed 36,000 people. The blast was heard 3,000 miles away. It was the loudest sound in recorded history.

COLD OUTSIDE, HOT INSIDE

Snow-covered Mount Shishaldin is one of 44 active volcanoes in Alaska. The United States has 54 active volcanoes, third in the world after Indonesia and Russia.

BOOM!

Washington's Mount St. Helens erupted in 1980. The blast blew the top off the volcano, sending rocks the size of school buses into the air.

SMASH!

The eruption at Mount St. Helens had the force of 500 atomic bombs. It flattened trees for 230 square miles.

41

6 Just Gorgeous

Mountains are exciting, but it's not easy to live on them. Most people live in flat areas—plains and plateaus (pla-TOHS). Plains, worn smooth by rivers and streams, are low. Often they are covered with grass. Plateaus are flat, too, but forces within the Earth have raised them high above the surrounding land. Sometimes rivers cut deep, sharp canyons, or gorges (GORJ-iz), into plateaus. This gives us such spectacular sights as the mile-deep Grand Canyon.

OLD OLDUVAI
Olduvai Gorge is part of the Great Rift Valley of Africa. This two-million-year-old valley appears where a plate is being pulled apart. Olduvai is almost 5,000 miles long.

WELCOME TO MARS
Stone needles and towers make Bryce Canyon, in Utah, look like another planet. These spiky rocks remained after rain, wind, and ice wore away softer rock and soil.

BIG BIGHORN
The Bighorn River winds its way through Bighorn Canyon in Wyoming. Canyons are usually wider at the top, or rim, where weather has helped wear soft rock away, and narrower at the bottom, where the river runs.

plateau

river

canyon

plateau

A BOOST FROM UNDERNEATH
Plateaus rise because colliding plates in the Earth push them from underneath, much as a giant hand might lift a table. When rivers cut through a rising plateau, they form canyons.

43

That's Grand

All it took was some dirty water and ten million years. Zap! The Grand Canyon! The Colorado River, filled with gritty sand and rock, carved this natural wonder out of the high Colorado Plateau. Today, the Grand Canyon drops a mile from rim to river at its deepest point.

WET AND WILD
Hang on! Five bold boaters take a wild ride down the Grand Canyon's Colorado River. Over hundreds of thousands of years, the rough and sandy waters of the Colorado carved the canyon through a plateau.

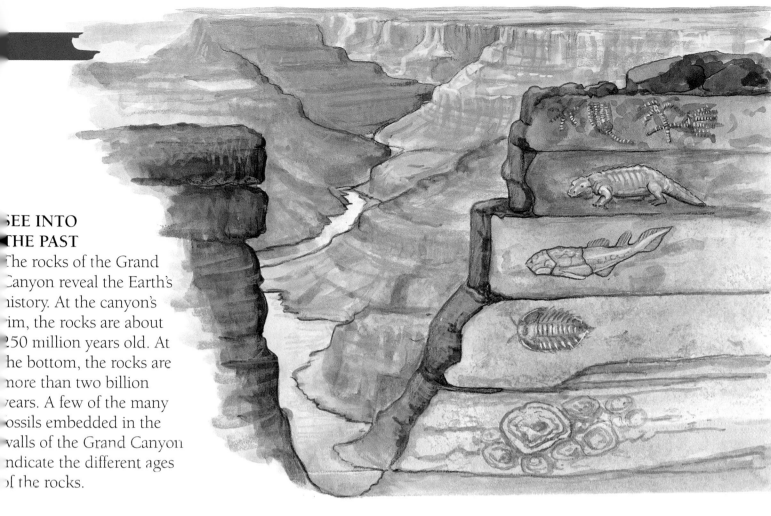

SEE INTO THE PAST

The rocks of the Grand Canyon reveal the Earth's history. At the canyon's rim, the rocks are about 250 million years old. At the bottom, the rocks are more than two billion years. A few of the many fossils embedded in the walls of the Grand Canyon indicate the different ages of the rocks.

crinoids:
250 million
years old

reptile:
250 million
years old

fish:
360 million
years old

trilobite:
500 million
years old

algae:
560 million
years old

WIDE OPEN SPACES

At its widest, the Grand Canyon is 18 miles from rim to rim. Wind, water, and plants have helped crumble away the canyon's rocks.

 Its Alive

Plants and animals live in almost every nook and cranny of the planet. They, like wind and water, change the shape of the Earth. Scientists break the world into four different regions based on the kinds of plants that grow there. The regions are forests, grasslands, deserts, and tundra.

DRY TIMES

Plants that grow in deserts are adapted to find and hold water. Some have wide root systems that grab rain after storms. Others have thick, fleshy stems that store water for drier times.

TREES GALORE

Aspen trees and evergreens, like these in Montana, grow in forest regions. Every continent except Antarctica contains forests.

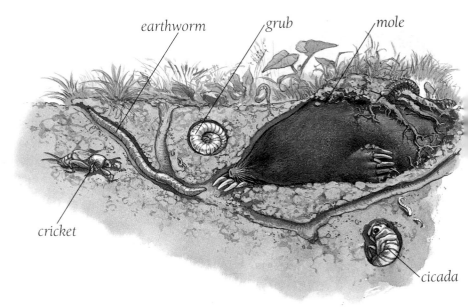

earthworm   grub   mole

cricket

cicada

DIRT MATTERS

Soil starts off as dead plants and pieces of rock. Then, living plants and animals break the plant remains and rock apart and stir the material around. It takes hundreds of years to make just a little soil.

GIANT STEPPES

A steppe (STEP) is not part of a staircase. Steppes are grasslands, like this one in Washington State. You can find them where winters are cold and summers are hot. Steppes are covered by short grasses, not much taller than one foot in height.

TOUGH TUNDRA

Tundra plants flower around Godhavn Harbor in Greenland. Tundra is a cold area with low-growing plants that bloom quickly when the weather warms up.

47

Forests

A forest is a big area covered with so many trees that their leaves shade the ground. Forests spread across almost one-third of the Earth's surface. They are divided into different types according to their leaves. The main types of forests are deciduous (dih-SIH-juh-wuhs) forests, rain forests, and evergreen forests.

A GOOD KIND OF LITTER
The floor of a deciduous forest can be thick with plant litter. Fallen leaves, old bark, and moss help to make the soil richer.

deer

fox

owl

opossum

mouse

turtle

HIDE AND SEEK
Forest animals hunt and hide within the shelter of trees.

◄ALL SPRUCED UP
Evergreen forests, like this spruce forest in Wyoming, grow in cool, damp places. Evergreen trees often have needle-like leaves that they keep all year.

SAY GOODBYE, LEAVES
The trees in deciduous forests, like this one in North Carolina, lose their leaves each year. Deciduous trees grow in areas with warm summers and cool winters.

WET AND WILD
Rain forests, such as this one in Australia, are usually wet and warm. They shelter a great variety of life. Almost half the Earth's plant and animal species are found in tropical rain forests.

49

Grasslands and Savannas

Grass, grass, everywhere, and hardly a tree in sight. That describes most grasslands. In places that get enough rain for grass to grow, but not enough for trees to survive, grasslands take over. North America's grasslands are its plains and prairies. African grasslands are called savannas. They are hot, dry, plains with small trees. In Argentina, the wide grasslands are called pampas (PAM-puz).

BIG PLAIN, BIG ANIMALS
The Serengeti Plain of East Africa is a typical savanna. Only a few small trees grow amid short and tall grasses. The Serengeti Plain supports many kinds of animals, among them giraffes, gazelles, wildebeests, and hyenas.

giraffes

hartebeests

rhinoceros

wildebeest

hyena

impala

cheetah

GLORIOUS GRASS
Pasqueflowers (PASK-flou-erz) dot the shortgrass prairie of North Dakota. Because their soil is rich, American grasslands have given way to farms in many places.

WHAT'S THAT RATTLING NOISE?
Back up carefully—this prairie rattlesnake is ready to strike! American grasslands shelter creatures from bison to prairie dogs.

51

Tundra

Tundra—a Russian word that means "high flat place"—is a cold area with low-growing plants. There are two kinds of tundra. Arctic tundra is found on land near the North and South Poles. Alpine tundra exists on high mountains. In both places, the weather is icy and the summers are short. Still, tundra plants grow back, year after year.

SKY-HIGH TUNDRA
Few plants can survive in the freezing temperatures of the highest Alpine tundra. In the Andes of Peru, only soft clumps of moss can live.

COVERED WITH COLOR
Millions of tiny plants called mosses, and plant-like organisms called lichen (LIKE-en) cling to the rocks of Signy Island, near Antarctica. These tough little life-forms are common in Arctic tundra.

As they migrate in the far north, caribou make a mea[l] from tiny tundra plants.

LAND OF SHORT PLANTS ▶
Trees cannot grow in the tundra of Manitoba, Canada. Instead, short grasses and small flowers hold on to the shallow soil. Although tundra plants can live through cold weather, in some ways they are delicate. Under th[e] thin soil of Arctic tundra, the ground is always frozen. Heavy trucks can hurt tundra soil and kill the plants.

52

8 What are These?

Have you ever seen shapes in the clouds? How about shapes in rock? All over the world, wind and water are wearing away stone. This process is called weathering. Sometimes the rock ends up looking like a familiar object—only huge. Perhaps you can guess the names, but a visitor from outer space would have to look in his guidebook to see what these formations are called.

SHEEP ROCK
Arches National Park, Utah

OLD MAN
Transvaal, Republic of
South Africa

CAMEL ROCK
Near Santa Fe,
New Mexico

ROCKY WOMAN
Kandersteg, Switzerland

ELEPHANT ROCK
Valley of Fire State Park, Nevada

55

Did You Know...

1" THAT the Sahara Desert of North Africa, now one of the hottest and driest places on Earth, was once green and wet? Prehistoric paintings and scientific studies show that the Sahara once had flowering trees and lakes. Elephants and giraffes used to live there.

2 **THAT** the legend of the sunken city of Atlantis may have started on the Greek island of Thera? A volcano once rose where this 1,000-foot-deep harbor is now. The mountain blew in 1500 B.C. The tidal wave that came after may have washed away a nearby civilization and inspired the story of the underwater city.

3 **THAT** the higher you climb, the colder it gets? Air temperature drops by 35.6° F for every 10,000 feet of elevation. Even in tropical countries, the tops of tall mountains are cold and wintry.

4 **THAT** Mauna Kea, a volcanic mountain in Hawaii, is taller than Mount Everest? Measured from sea level, Mauna Kea is only 13,796 feet high. However, the volcano rises from the ocean floor. Measured from the bottom of the Pacific, it is 33,476 feet tall—almost a mile higher than Everest.

5 **THAT** the mighty Amazon River contains almost one fifth of all the river water in the world? Fresh water from the Amazon can be found 113 miles out to sea.

BRAZIL
113

6 **THAT** Angel Falls in Venezuela is named not after an angel, but a prospector? In 1935 an American named Jimmy Angel was looking for gold when he spotted this towering torrent. It turned out to be the tallest waterfall in the world, with a drop of 3,212 feet straight down.

Glossary

ATOLL A low, ring-shaped coral island.

CANYON A deep valley with steep sides, often with a stream running through it.

CONTINENT One of the main divisions of land on Earth. The seven continents are Asia, Africa, North America, South America, Antarctica, Europe, and Australia.

CORE The hot, innermost layer of the Earth.

CRUST The rocky, outermost layer of the Earth.

DELTA A flat plain that forms at the mouth of a river.

FAULT A break in the Earth's crust along which great masses of rock move.

GEYSER A hot spring through which jets of water and steam erupt.

GLACIER A mass of ice that moves slowly over land.

GORGE A deep, narrow valley whose sides are almost straight up and down. A gorge is usually smaller than a canyon.

IGNEOUS Made from the hot, melted rock called magma.

LAVA Hot, melted rock that flows onto the Earth's surface.

MAGMA Hot, melted rock within the Earth.

MANTLE The middle layer of the Earth, made of hot rock.

METAMORPHIC Changed in shape or structure by heat and pressure.

PLATE One of many huge, rocky slabs that make up the outer shell of the Earth.

PLATEAU A large, flat area that is higher than the surrounding land.

SAVANNA A tropical grassland containing scattered trees.

SEDIMENTARY Formed from layers of sediment—small pieces of rock and plant and animal remains.

STEPPE Grassland, covered by short grasses, that occurs where there are distinct seasons.

TUNDRA A cold land found in Arctic regions or mountains that is covered with low plants.

VEGETATION All the plants in one area.

VOLCANO A vent in the Earth through which lava, ashes, and gases erupt. A volcano often takes the form of a mountain or hill around such a vent.

WATER TABLE The part of the ground closest to the surface that is filled with water.

WEATHERING The breaking down of rocks by water, ice, acids, plants, and changes in temperature.

Credits

crystal

Published by
The National Geographic Society
Reg Murphy, *President and Chief Executive Officer*
Gilbert M. Grosvenor, *Chairman of the Board*
Nina D. Hoffman, *Senior Vice President*
William R. Gray, *Vice President and Director, Book Division*

Staff for this Book
Barbara Lalicki, *Director of Children's Publishing*
Barbara Brownell, *Senior Editor and Project Manager*
Marianne R. Koszorus, *Senior Art Director and Project Manager*
Toni Eugene, *Editor*
Alexandra Littlehales, *Art Director*
Susan V. Kelly, *Illustrations Editor*
Patricia Daniels, *Researcher*
Carl Mehler, *Senior Map Editor*
Jennifer Emmett, *Assistant Editor*
Meredith Wilcox, *Illustrations Assistant*
Dale-Marie Herring, *Administrative Assistant*
Elisabeth MacRae-Bobynskyj, *Indexer*
Mark A. Caraluzzi, *Marketing Manager*
Vincent P. Ryan, *Manufacturing Manager*
Lewis R. Bassford, *Production Project Manager*

Acknowledgments

We are grateful for the assistance of Peter B. Stifel, Ph.D., *Scientific Consultant*. We also thank John Agnone and Rebecca Lescaze, National Geographic Book Division, for their guidance and suggestions.

Illustrations Credits

COVER Adam Jones/Planet Earth Pictures
Interior Photographs from the Earth Scenes Division of Animals Animals Enterprises.
Front Matter: 1 David J. Boyle. 2-3 Peter Weimann. 4 (top to bottom), Breck P. Kent, Bates Littlehales, M. A. Chappell, Betty K. Bruce. 5 (top to bottom), Harold E. Wilson, Bates Littlehales, Patti Murray. 6-7 (art), Warren Cutler. 8 (map), Jehan Aziz. 8 Breck P. Kent. 9 (upper), Hjalmar R. Bardarson; (lower left), Henry Ausloos; (lower right), Breck P. Kent. 10 (art), Robert Cremins. 10-11 (all), Breck P. Kent. 12 (art), Robert Cremins. 12 (left), Ken Cole; (right), Fabio Colombini. 13 (upper), Jim Tuten; (lower) David Welling.
The Deep Blue Sea: 14 Brian Milne. 15 (art), Warren Cutler. 15 (left), Henry Ausloos; (right), Rich Reid. 16 (art), Robert Cremins. 16 (left), Bates Littlehales; (right), David B. Fleetham/OSF. 17 Robert Maier. 18-19 (art), Robert Cremins.
Islands: 20 (art,) Robert Cremins, 20 David M. Barron. 21 (art), Warren Cutler. 21 Michael Fredericks 22 (art), Robert Cremins. 22 Breck P. Kent. 23 David C. Fritts.
Waterworks: 24 (art), Robert Cremins. 24-25 Raj Kamal/OSF. 25 (art), Warren Cutler. 26 (art left), Warren Cutler; (art right), Robert Cremins. 26 (upper), Photosafari (PVT) Ltd.; (lower), C.C. Lockwood. 27 (art), Warren Cutler. 27 E.R. Degginger. 28 (art), Robert Cremins. 28 Stefan Meyers GDT. 29 Richard Packwood/OSF. 30 (art, upper), Robert Cremins; (art, lower), Warren Cutler. 30 Johnny Johnson. 31 M.A. Chappell.
Dry Spells: 32 (art), Robert Cremins. 32 (both), Breck P. Kent. 33 (art), Robert Cremins. 33 John Gerlach. 34 (art), Robert Cremins. 34 (upper right), Michael Fogden; (middle), Anthony Bannister; (lower), Mark Stouffer. 35 (art), Warren Cutler. 35 Betty K. Bruce.
Mountains: 36 (art), Warren Cutler. 36 Phil Degginger. 37 (art), Robert Cremins. 37 (upper), Michael P. Gadomski; (lower), Zig Leszczynski. 38 (art), Robert Cremins. 38 (upper), Ben Osborne/OSF; (lower), Doug Allan/OSF. 39 (art), Warren Cutler. 39 Martyn Colbect/OSF. 40 E.R. Degginger. 41 (art), Warren Cutler. 41 (upper left), Anne Head; (lower left), John Stern; (right), Harold E. Wilson.
Just Gorgeous: 42 (upper), Tom Leach/OSF; (lower), Ken Cole. 43 (art), Warren Cutler. 43 E. R. Degginger. 44-45 (both), C.C. Lockwood. 45 (art), Warren Cutler.
It's Alive: 46 (art), Robert Cremins. 46 (left), Bates Littlehales; (right), E.R. Degginger. 47 (upper), Doug Wechsler; (lower), S.R. Morris/OSF. 48 (upper), David J. Boyle; (lower), Bates Littlehales. 49 (art), Robert Cremins. 49 (upper), Bates Littlehales; (lower), Keith Gillett. 50 (art), Robert Cremins. 51 (both), Bates Littlehales. 52 (art), Robert Cremins. 52 (left), Doug Allan/OSF; (right), Breck P. Kent. 53 Bates Littlehales.
What Are These?: 54 (top to bottom), David J. Boyle, Leen Van Der Slik, John Lemker. 55 (left), Patti Murray; (right), Peter W. Baumann.
Back Matter: 56 (art), Robert Cremins. 56 (top), Mike Andrews; (bottom), Alan Fortune. 57 (art, upper), Warren Cutler, (art, lower), Robert Cremins. 57 David Welling. 60 Breck P. Kent.

COVER: Stripe patterns, called crossbeds, line sandstone in Utah Sandstone is a type of sedimentary rock.

Composition for this book by the National Geographic Society Book Division. Printed and bound by R.R. Donnelley & Sons Company, Willard, Ohio. Color separations by NEC, Nashville, Tennessee. Case cover printed by Inland Press, Menomonee Falls, Wisconsin.

Library of Congress CIP Data
Daniels, Patricia, 1955-
    Earth / by Patricia Daniels.
        p.   cm   — (National Geographic nature library)
    Includes index.
    Summary: Examines the composition and surface characteristics of the Earth, describing such features as rivers, mountains and other land formations, and various vegetative regions.
    ISBN 0-7922-7046-0
    1. Earth sciences—Juvenile literature. 2. Earth—Juvenile literature.   [1.Earth.]   I. Title.   II. Series
QE29.D325   1998
550—dc21   97-27748
                                                                    CIP
                                                                    AC